Zion Canyon

Gregory McNamee, SERIES EDITOR

Zion Canyon

A Storied Land

TEXT BY Greer K. Chesher

PHOTOGRAPHS BY Michael Plyler

The University of Arizona Press   Tucson

This book is dedicated to
the memory of Ellen Meloy and Anton Gehring.
The world and I miss you both.

The University of Arizona Press
Text © 2007 Greer K. Chesher
Photographs © 2007 Michael Plyler
All rights reserved
This book is printed on acid-free, archival-quality paper.
Manufactured in the United States of America

12 11 10 09 08 07   6 5 4 3 2 1

Library of Congress Cataloging-in-Publication Data appear
on the last printed page of this book.

Frontispiece: Toward a Unique Personal Vision

contents

photographs

PHOTOGRAPHS

X

acknowledgments

I'd like to thank the following individuals for their help and support in the writing of this manuscript. I couldn't have done it without you. Well, I could have, but it wouldn't have been a tenth as good or as fun—thanks! Jack Burns, Zion National Park; Dr. Lynne Cobb, St. George, Utah; J. L. Crawford and Elva Twitchell of Zion Canyon, and all the folks who shared their lives with me as part of the Pioneer Voices of Zion Canyon Oral History Project; Dr. Tim B. Graham, U.S. Geological Survey, Canyonlands Field Station, Moab, Utah; Dr. Wayne Hamilton, Springdale, Utah; Sharon and David Hatfield,

Rockville, Utah; Polly Hays, Denver, Colorado; Teresa Jordan, Salt Lake City, Utah; Dr. Harry Kurtz, Jr., Clemson University, Clemson, South Carolina; Gregory McNamee, Tucson, Arizona; Ellen Meloy, the World; Michael Plyler, Springdale, Utah; Dr. Richard Segal, Midvale, Utah; Sandra Scott, Irving, Texas. Any misinterpretations are my own.

Zion Canyon

The ephemeral Sinawava Falls and The Pulpit

introduction: the language of Zion

Not long ago I sat in a small-town diner not far from here eating a small-town breakfast of fried eggs and hash browns when the European couple in the next booth waved the waitress over. A writer's job is to pay attention, and so I did, my ears growing like Pinocchio's nose. I unstuck my legs from the vinyl seat and scooted forward for a better view as the young, blonde daughter of the cook and owner bobbed to the couple's table.

"Do you have any stronger coffee?" the man implored through a thick accent, tilting his still-full cup toward her, its contents a translucent brown.

"Ahhh," she replied, "let me ask my mom."

Away she trotted to the kitchen, and I couldn't wait to see with what she would return. I was debating whether she had ever heard of espresso, something these folks probably injected, when she returned and smiling widely, said, "Here! Use as much as you like!" She triumphantly set a scoop of instant coffee crystals, tastefully presented in a small white bowl, on their table and whirled away. The couple leaned forward, stared at each other, then the bowl, and tentatively poked it with a spoon.

This is the Utah, and the Zion, I love.

Zion is its own country with its own language. This used to be truer than it is now. There was a time when everyone spoke with a drawl, a southern twang almost, a western accent only heard now on the remotest ranches or from the oldest speakers. There are still young people, men mostly, who lean on their faded pickups in skinny-legged jeans, long-sleeved shirts buttoned at wrist and neck, and crisp cowboy hats who drawl into the long day about *bobwyr fentces, pert near everbody,* and *upta,* as in "I'm going *upta* Cedar City." But the influx of "accentless," English-speaking newcomers is changing all that.

Years ago I recall looking up a mystery plant *everbody* called *Sarvis berry.* It turned out to be the familiar serviceberry. I had to learn to pronounce Cedar City, not with the accent on the word city, but as *CEE-dercity.* The nearby town of Hurricane is not pronounced like a tropical storm, but as a word with its own force: *HURR-i-cun.* I had to learn to call junipers cedars and to say such things as "Oh for cute!" and "Oh my heck!" in polite company.

Language reveals much. And with it goes much more. A nuance of meaning, particularities of place, a way of inhabiting the world. Words evolve to fit a place, pronunciations become angled by cliff echoes, sharpened by rockfall, smoothed by water.

Who knows what delicate shades of meaning were lost with the Virgin Anasazi and Parowan Fremont tongues. Maybe they're preserved in the Tiwa, Tewa, Towa, Keres, Hopi, or Zuni languages still in use in Arizona and New Mexico's extant pueblos. The Virgin Anasazi and Parowan Fremont lived in and around Zion, on the Colorado Plateau's fringe, their world's western extent, looking out over western Utah and Nevada's Basin and Range province. I imagine they spoke words created by canyons, and those same canyons were brought to life by words. A people and language shaped by environment. I imagine Anasazi as a language of water—water dripping, water running, water falling, water talking. I hear it often.

Other languages existed here. We see them reflected in the canyon's names. The Paiute called it Mukuntuweap, the original meaning now obscure. There is Parunuweap Canyon ("a canyon with a swift stream"), the Pa'rus Trail (*PA-roos,* "white foaming water"; Parussi, "whirling water," the Virgin River), Mount Kinesava, and the Temple of Sinawava (in the Paiute creation story, heroes Wolf and Coyote are called Senangwav, a name that also translates as "God" or "Spirit").

Pioneer names resonate in places such as Behunin and Heaps Canyons, Crawford Wash, and Johnson Mountain. In 1916 Frederick Vining Fisher, a Methodist missionary and national park advocate, named the Great White

Throne (God's Throne) and, with his local guide Claud Hirschi, the Three Patriarchs. The Mormon faith echoes in Mount Moroni and Kolob Canyons. Zion, a word interpreted around these parts as "sanctuary," is borrowed from Hebrew.

Names reveal a history and a worldview. There are the practical: Horse Pasture Plateau and Corral Hollow; the directional: North and South Guardian Angel, East and West Temple; the descriptive: Pine Valley, Grapevine Spring, Wildcat Canyon, Coalpits Wash. In such beautiful places people often revert to the language of awe and grandeur: Mount Majesty, Castle Dome, Inclined Temple, Phantom Valley, Mountain of Mystery. And there are the unknown: LaVerkin Wash. LaVerkin? Nobody knows. What would we call the Great White Throne today?

Some Paiute call their homeland Tiwiinarivipi, the "Storied Land." In an ethnographic overview of Zion National Park, Paiute Angelita Bullets says, "It is said that the plants, animals, and in fact, everything on this land, understands the Paiute language, and when one listens closely and intently enough, there is affirmation and a sense of understanding. The complexity of our culture lies in our ability to converse with the animals and the landscape in this land. It is believed that this ability will prove to be important for all mankind someday." The land, it is said, understands us. It is speaking to us all the time. The late Paiute Elder Clifford Jake said, "The land is waiting for our answer."

I want to tell you of this Zion. Of a land that speaks, that sings. I want you to hear the song of cottonwood whispering to the Virgin's waters. I

Checkerboard Mesa and Clear Creek drainage

Clifford Jake

want you to see the color of sunset on the cliffs in fall. I feel my language inadequate.

To tell you the story of Zion, to have you feel it, see it, I want a different way of talking, a new alphabet. I want a language full of exacting definition: a word for the precise pink of manzanita flowers in earliest spring, for the experimental green of cottonwoods leafing along the Virgin River, itself the dusty watercolor of spring runoff.

I want a word to convey the first touch of sun hot on winter-white flesh so you can feel it, smell it. Scratch-and-sniff words; hot words and cold; words jagged as a new-broken rockfall. Words that lie smooth as a water-worn pebble in your mind.

I want ink that, when held up to the light, glows like melon cut open in the sun, like light through a cactus petal. Ink that, when read, splashes off the page, river water around boulders. I want parchment the color of Indian ricegrass in June. I want a language of thunderstorm and baked sand.

I can only acquaint you with the conversation I've been having with this place for the last twenty years or so, and I can only use the language I have, inadequate though it may be. I carry a slight accent. Those from here can tell I'm not, but they can also tell that after all these years I am now *of* here.

Zion converses with mockingbird and desert tortoise, mountain lion and morning cloak. It twirls cliffrose plumes on its windy fingers while waiting to speak with you. Get yourself a cuppa coffee; let's talk.

the many Zions

I am sitting in my studio. On the broad oak desk before me lies my writerly equipment, five maps—Utah, southern Utah, southwestern Utah, Zion National Park, a Zion topographic map—and a steaming cup of mocha, just brewed. I draw ever-tightening circles on these maps, homing in on Zion. Every now and then, I glance out the windows above my desk, take a sip of coffee, and see it there, this Zion I seek on paper. Outside, my small orchard blooms pink and white against cliffs bathed red in morning light. My eyes can't help but be drawn upward to the overarching greatness of sky, turquoise against terra-cotta. This is my Zion, my personal haven, embraced by these redrock walls, under this particular reach of blue.

There are many Zions, though most people will tell you it is a deep, redrock canyon cut into southwestern Utah's Navajo Sandstone: Zion Canyon. But Zion is something much bigger, and something much harder to put one's finger on than a map's concentrated contours.

There is the geographic Zion: a region enclosed by Highway 14 on the north, Interstate 15 on the west, Highways 59 and 389 on the south, and Highway 89 on the east. These roads make convenient boundaries because they reveal the region's geography. Highway 14 strikes across the Markagunt Plateau's high country, the head of the Zion-defining Virgin River and its tributaries. Interstate 15 runs along the Hurricane Fault, the Colorado Plateau's western edge atop which Zion perches. Highways 59 and 389 skirt the Vermilion Cliffs, the bounds of Zion's particular flora and fauna mix. Highway 89 snakes up the Sevier Fault, separating the Zion-carrying Markagunt Plateau from the Bryce-holding Paunsaugunt Plateau. I would fine-tune this description to include, as a southeast boundary, the nameless road that runs from Highway 389 past Coral Pink Sand Dunes State Park and through Yellowjacket Canyon to Highway 89 near Mount Carmel Junction. These borders capture the high-country beginnings and low-country results of the waters, canyons, and lives of Zion.

Zion is easily defined geologically: where the Virgin River carves deep redrock canyons into the Colorado Plateau's Navajo Sandstone. Although the details are complex (there are actually nine geologic layers revealed in Zion), this story is simply told: high-country precipitation rushes downhill, cutting canyons. This is a universal story, but nowhere on earth do the results look exactly like this—this river, this rock.

There is the political Zion: Zion National Park, an area much smaller than those described above. Initially, Zion Canyon was set aside as Mukuntuweap National Monument in 1909 by President William Howard Taft, who invoked the Antiquities Act, the same act President Clinton used to such controversy to establish Grand Staircase–Escalante National Monument in 1996. In 1918, the name was changed to Zion National Monument, and in 1919, the monument was expanded and protected as a national park by an act of Congress. In 1937, a nearby section of Navajo Sandstone hewn by a Virgin River tributary (LaVerkin Creek), the Kolob Canyons, was established as a separate national monument and, in 1956, added to Zion National Park. The park now totals 146,597 acres (229 square miles), of which 90 percent has been recommended to Congress for protection as a designated wilderness area.

In the old days, nice straight borders were drawn around scenic wonders without regard to their biotic workings. So Zion National Park's boundaries decapitate headwaters, leaving the park vulnerable to upstream forces. If Zion were drawn today, instead of looking on a map like stacked blocks, it might morph amoebalike around drainages and highlands. Perhaps early park planners thought the Virgin's thousand-foot headwater chasms were so inaccessible as to be safe. But water in the desert is never safe.

It wasn't until 1996 that the Department of the Interior, in a precedent-setting agreement with the state of Utah, finally negotiated federal reserved instream water rights for Zion National Park. Such rights secure instream flows, defined as streamflows that sustain native riverine species, aquatic and riparian communities, and natural ecosystem functions. What would Zion be without these? In this same negotiation, the state relinquished two proposed dam sites upstream on the Virgin's North and East Forks in trade for a large dam and reservoir downstream in Sand Hollow near Hurricane, Utah. This was the first time Utah recognized water rights for anything but agriculture or development. The idea did not exist that rivers needed water just to be rivers.

In 2004, 2.7 million people visited Zion National Park. That's eleven thousand visitors per day during the peak months of July and August. Between mid-1980 and 2000, annual visitation nearly doubled. And with southwestern Utah's population soaring, it's hard to imagine what Zion might look like in another twenty years. Already the main canyon drive is closed to passenger cars from April through October; buses now shuttle visitors to popular destinations.

Then there is the canyon itself, what most people might call Zion: a canyon roughly twenty-five miles long from the North Fork's head to its mouth near Rockville, Utah. Most folks are familiar only with the eight miles from the National Park Service Visitor Center to the end of the scenic drive at the Temple of Sinawava, along which red Navajo Sandstone walls soar two to three thousand feet above the canyon floor.

There is the biotic Zion, which, in my mind, corresponds roughly with

Zion's larger geographic boundaries—a Greater Zion Ecosystem, if you will. Zion is a complex landscape, or better, a landscape of complexities. Zion's geographical boundaries also define ecosystem change; it is defined by what's without as well as what's within. To the west, Highway 15 flanks the Colorado Plateau's abrupt escarpment and separates plateau biota from that of the Mojave and Great Basin Deserts. Highway 14 skirts the montane north. In the south, Highway 389 drops to the hotter, lower Uinkaret Plateau. And in the east, Highway 89 separates Kanab's sand dune deserts from Zion's sandstone canyons.

Tucked in niches, hidden in soil, peeking from cliffs, and skittering between our feet, an amazing array of plants and animals—from tiny piñon mice to golden eagles and mountain lion—thrive in Zion's many habitats. The park's elevational range, from 3,600 to 8,700 feet, allows vastly different environments. Fir, pine, and aspen prefer the high country's snowy winters, while piñon, cliffrose, and mesquite flourish in the desert's heat.

Water, and the lack of it, decides what grows where. On the plateau, above the canyon rim, annual precipitation tops twenty-six inches. In this relatively cool, moist environment, sego lilies sprout under greenleaf manzanita, yellow-bellied marmots scurry between white fir, and reintroduced elk mix with black bear.

In the desert, the Virgin River's perennial waters give life to an overstory of Fremont cottonwood, singleleaf ash, and box elder. The rare Zion snail lives only in Zion's isolated hanging gardens, which grow lush with maidenhair fern, scarlet monkey flower, and golden columbine. Canyon treefrogs bleat

Desert marsh

while campers sleep, and great blue herons wade the river's currents. When summer monsoons send flash floods roaring down canyon, it's a testimony to the idea of survival of the fittest that anything survives at all.

That's also true away from the river, where aridity has real meaning. In Zion Canyon, annual precipitation may total a mere fourteen inches. At the lowest elevations, Mojave Desert species—banded Gila monsters and honey mesquite—infiltrate Zion's dry, south-facing canyons. At mid-elevations, Great Basin Desert species such as shadscale and big sagebrush mingle with the Colorado Plateau's bigtooth maple and Utah juniper. But Zion's biotic diversity far exceeds that of these nearby desert ecosystems.

Part of Zion's uniqueness comes from its substrates. Great Basin and Mojave Desert soils tend to be monotonously uniform over great distances. But Zion's stacked prehistoric environments erode into many soils. For example, the Chinle Formation's ancient lakes and volcanic ash corrode into a soil rich in the poisonous element selenium. Specialized plants—prince's plume and twelve species of milkvetch (also known as locoweed from the affects of its selenium-infused leaves), for instance—grow on such soils and increase Zion's diversity. Individual and unconnected canyons also increase diversity as isolation creates new species.

We can talk about high-country and low-country, desert and riparian ecosystems as if they were separate entities, but this misses the integration of the whole. When we draw a circle on a map and include disparate environments, there must be something that unifies, that makes this place uniquely Zion. Perhaps that interior unity is beyond our naming. For example, biologists once thought DNA directed an organism's every detail. But, according to the Human Genome Project, it turns out that people don't have enough genes (not many more than a roundworm) to explain the body's astounding intricacy. Biologists now think "organizational" or "emergent" principles somehow kick in at larger sizes. Sort of like the sum is greater than its parts, and not predictable by examining any part. Here is my point: it is the particular organization of the Zion ecosystem that accounts for its uniqueness; that there is an (or many overlapping) emergent principle(s) at work. The danger in any organization has always been tampering with individual elements. Take out an appendix, no big deal. Half a liver, a spleen, a lung, a kidney; who cares? A pancreas, a heart, oops, we're over the edge. Remove mountain lions, bighorn sheep, black bears, wolves, spotted owls, peregrine falcons, Virgin River spinedace; when do we cross the line? When do the emergent principles fail? When do we no longer have Zion?

Then there is the cultural Zion: a nine- to eleven-thousand-year history of peoples moving across and interacting with this landscape, from Paleo- and Archaic peoples to Ancestral Puebloans (known by archaeologists as the Virgin Branch of the Anasazi and the Parowan Fremont), and Southern Paiute to modern Euro-Americans. Here are settlements prehistoric, historic, and modern, where people long raised children and food, fought floods and sometimes each other, and imbibed the time's popular hot beverage. There are Mormon towns, present and past—Springdale, Rockville, Adventure, Grafton, Northup, and Shunesburg. Only two (Springdale and Rockville) still hold living people, but all are discussed as if they still exist, as they do

The Sentinel in winter

in their descendants' memories. This idea reminds me of a Hopi concept: ancient pueblos are not abandoned ruins but home signs. They say, "We still inhabit that place. Even if we no longer live there, our ancestors do." The Paiute feel the same about traditional lands. It seems no matter where we are from, our roots hold soil. Zion is a human landscape where certain stories, grounded in the land, are told.

There is the Zion of the man who named it, a place of freedom from religious persecution.

There is the physical reality and, for those who feel it, the emotional response—the Zion of the heart and mind. The Zion we carry with us. Each of us, depending on our own history and view, looks at Zion and sees a different story. Let me tell you a couple stories the Zion I know told me.

a Zion story in two languages

THIS IS HOW CANYONS FORM (TEXTBOOK)

Two dominant erosional processes combine to form the canyons of Zion National Park: downcutting and canyon widening. The relatively homogeneous Navajo Sandstone is soft enough to be easily eroded but strong enough to stand in tall, vertical cliffs. The Virgin River acts like a moving ribbon of sandpaper transporting an average of 3,657 tons or 366 dump-truck loads of sediment per day.

The process of canyon widening becomes important below the Navajo Sandstone. The relatively soft Kayenta Formation is more easily eroded than the overlying Navajo Sandstone. As the Kayenta erodes and slips away in landslides, the great cliffs of Navajo Sandstone are undermined and, despite their inherent strength, eventually break away. Rockfalls and landslides are thus an important part of the canyon-widening process.

—adapted from *Geology of Utah's Parks and Monuments*

THIS IS HOW CANYONS FORM (REALITY)

Overhead the early morning sky stretches, spotless and cerulean. Flies buzz in the dry, late summer stillness. It's a long eleven miles to our camp on this overnight trek through the narrow, trail-less Right Fork of North Creek—over boulders, around pouroffs, down scree, up talus, at least six rappels with full packs, and frigid, stagnant lagoons in sunless narrows with names such as the Black Pool. Unbeknownst to us, it is going to be a very long day—and an even longer night. Canyons will widen, slots will deepen. A river of liquid sandpaper howling like a freight train is about to ship a few hundred boxcars of sediment through this canyon without regard to its human cargo.

Six of us, park rangers on a busman's holiday, stand atop 7,890-foot Lava Point in Zion's backcountry and survey our domain. We are five women and one man: two backcountry rangers, Jon and Janet; and four interpretive rangers or, in park service jargon, naturalists, Polly, Candace, Marta, and me. (However, if you're European, a naturalist is what we in the United States call a nudist. Now, I have also on occasion been that, but right now I'm talking about a job title.) Like any interpreter, we speak a language foreign or at least unintelligible to many: we speak nature; we interpret landscape. So, looking out over this vast terrain we see not only a stunning view, where, to the north, a lava-strewn slope ramps up to a pine-topped plateau, but also underlying structure and its meaning: here southern Utah's Markagunt Plateau perches atop the Colorado Plateau. This elevational redoubling is important, for without it, Zion's redrock canyons would not be.

Fifteen million years ago, the Pacific Plate's subduction under California pushed the Colorado Plateau, that great land block stretching from southern Colorado, to northern New Mexico, northern Arizona, and southern Utah, to a median elevation of 10,000 feet. A mere one to two million years ago, the Hurricane Fault, slipping by just west of Zion and east of St. George, hiked the Markagunt Plateau even higher. Add to that a few fault-rimming volcanoes and some sediment-capping lava flows, and we get the ponderosa-clad Markagunt's 11,000-foot heights.

To the west, in the Great Basin, sere clouds off the Sierra Nevada suck what little moisture remains from the desert and blow gently east on prevailing winds. The Markagunt's high point, 11,315-foot Brian Head, snags their swollen gray bellies. Here, winter snows pile amid towering spruce, fir, and aspen before melting into canyon-cutting spring runoff. At this elevation, water equals tremendous cutting power once unleashed downhill.

Water running off Cedar Mountain to the west carves Cedar Breaks National Monument's brilliant formations and Ashdown Gorge Wilderness

Area's deep gash. Water running off the gentle north and eastern slopes creates Panguitch Lake and the north-flowing Sevier (pronounced not like the French, but like a comment on the landscape—*sa-VERE*) River. Water running south, ah, well, water running south seeps into cooled volcanic embers, drips in chambers, runs through tubes until bursting from a black cliff like fire from a hose. The Virgin River, contrary to her name, is not born of grace but from a devil's cauldron. Like molten rock before her, the Virgin's waters run and spread from the plateau, fingering cracks, filing declivities, pouring through time and the lay of the land.

To the south, Zion National Park lies open before us. Narrow canyons slice the plateau into myriad freestanding mesas. Zion lies along the course of the Virgin River and its tributaries, basically the path snowmelt takes from the Markagunt to the Pacific. Along the way, the Virgin drainage dissects a thick block of ancient sand, the Navajo Sandstone, creating spectacular sheer redrock canyons. The Virgin and her preeminent canyon, Zion, are not alone; tributary canyons—East Fork, Orderville Gulch, Kolob, Crystal, and Deep Creeks—splay on a map like a bare-branched juniper. Shift your gaze a map's length west, and another branching tributary sucks rock from dry land, creating another Zion Canyon's worth of beauty, this time Great West Canyon. West again, and it's LaVerkin Creek creating the Kolob Canyons. Outside the park, the Virgin creates one last master canyon, the Virgin River Gorge, before she buries her head in the Colorado River in Lake Mead's Overton Arm. Given any chance to run downhill, the Virgin gouges great creases into mountain flanks in the effortless effort of water seeking the sea.

People often talk about *Bryce, Zion, and Grand Canyon* like a Holy Trinity of parks; these are the must-sees on any tourist itinerary. But, in actuality, to understand Zion we need to shift a tad west and talk about a different triad: *Cedar Breaks, Zion, and Lake Mead.* These are the links in the water chain.

This canyon cutting, at only two million years old, is relatively new. Geologists now think that the bulk of canyon cutting occurred extremely recently, during the Pleistocene's heavy runoff, when wetter climates or melting ice sent increased water coursing downstream. It was not the gradual, relentless work of today's relatively tiny (one hundred cubic feet per second average) Virgin River, but the gouging of greater waters that carved Zion's canyons. Water makes quick work of the homogeneous Navajo Sandstone, leaving only a slot until reaching lower, softer layers. Thus, many of Zion's canyons are extremely narrow. Zion Canyon itself, at its narrowest, is only sixteen feet wide and a thousand feet deep; backcountry canyons cut by smaller, ephemeral streams are even narrower. It is into one of these sharp, knife thrusts of a canyon that we head.

All this talk about elevation, water, and sandstone's relative sturdiness may seem academic, but tonight, glued to a ledge barely the size of my butt, I will understand geology's sovereignty. Historian Will Durant supposedly said that "civilization exists by geological consent, subject to change without notice" (anonymous). Little do I know that only by geological consent will we exist tomorrow.

Beneath our feet, the hardpan barely scuffs as we file from Lava Point along the West Rim Trail in early light. At this high elevation the sun is hot

Slickrock below the rim, Petroglyph Canyon

enough to bend shoulders, but the cool dryness wicks sweat. Turning toward Wildcat Canyon, the open glade of tall ponderosa, bunched Gambel oak, and toe-catching lava breaks away into a maze of deep, white-rimmed, redrock canyons. The high country is dry, but green lushness accompanies us along the Wildcat Canyon Trail: elderberry, the spent stalks of elkweed, serviceberry, the last sunflowers, the juniper-purple of Oregon grape, goldenrod, and bracken fern, all encased in an astounding quiet. We pause to take it in and point out our route: down Wildcat Canyon, across Left Fork of North Creek, over a steep, sandy saddle to the head of the Right Fork drainage. It's the last we'll see of the long view. The narrow canyons below are worlds of their own.

We enter Wildcat Canyon high and bushwhack down, first through stiff mountain mahogany and bristling oak, then leafy maples, aspen, and wild rose. We think we're clear as we head across open white slickrock littered with ball-bearing iron concretions that locals call "Moqui marbles" until the route swings back through the manzanita-choked, thigh-ripping stream course. Thousand-foot Navajo Sandstone walls surround us, the color of bone. Ledgy, quarter-inch sandstone striations, the sweeping fingerprints of fossil winds, crumble underfoot. Navajo Sandstone represents the largest known desert to grace the planet. During the early Jurassic (192 to 178 million years ago), sand piled at least 2,200-feet thick over 150,000 square miles from what's now Wyoming to southern California, Utah, and New Mexico. Back then these states were just sixteen degrees north of the equator, much like the Sahara today. (Interestingly, Sahara, an Arabic word, means not only desert but also ocean—a generic word meaning something like "the big empty").

The sands, blown one way and then another across this vast erg, or sand sea, ossified under the pressure and chemical influence of an advancing ocean. But the Navajo's strong patterns, the fossilized cross-beds of drifting dunes, look today as if they could whirl away again on the next strong breeze.

Scientists now think the Navajo Sandstone's sand is the eroded remains of the Appalachian Mountains transported across the continent on a massive, westward-flowing, long-gone river system to a point somewhere northwest of what's now Zion. Then, the northwesterlies started blowing for, oh, fifteen million years or so, and all that sand piled here before turning to stone. It's still on the move as southern Utah's redrock erodes into its constituent sand, blows away, and collects in a narrow notch in the Vermilion Cliffs near Kanab at Coral Pink Sand Dunes State Park or at Sand Mountain near Hurricane. We may look at Zion's redrock cliffs and wax eloquent about permanence and eternity, but the entire place is on the move.

Where intermittent streams run, the Navajo's tiny ledges melt into smooth chutes. Everywhere, eroding sand veneers slickrock, and we slip and slide down a path of little resistance. The canyon funnels gradually, forcing us to the lip of a twenty-foot pouroff where the Navajo Sandstone changes from white to red. We enter the sheer walls below in a way not necessarily advisable or even smart, but at least quick: bear-hugging a sapling ponderosa and launching ourselves, one-by-one over the rim, riding the pine's limber arc to the ground.

From Wildcat we traverse a long, dry ridgeline and stare into the shadowy depths of a canyon we must cross, Left Fork of North Creek. We climb down

Navajo Sandstone striations

its loose, forested slope—too steep to walk and too moderate to rappel—on a shoestring, rapping off a tree trunk and traversing the rope's full length before discovering we've miscalculated. Mapless, but with the optimism of young, unscarred rangers, we cast the rope over a ridge, where, we discover too late, it ends midpitch. Shoe-skiing the last couple hundred feet, gripping and stripping serviceberries and Douglas firs of leaves and needles, digging heels and fingernails in the powdery dirt to slow our descent, we arrive at last, raw-knuckled and skinned-kneed, in the cool silence of the Left Fork of North Creek. Readjusting packs and egos, we walk in the cool shade of canyon walls, replenished by the smell of water and peat. In round-backed alcoves, seep water drips from nodding maidenhair fern. From somewhere down canyon, that most hallowed of desert sounds comes: the hush of water over rock.

Narrow canyons are Edens of dim light, sinuous redrock, and the most coveted thing for which there is no Commandment (though plenty of covenants), desert water. This is a universal passion. People, by the thousands, stumble into the visitor centers at Grand Canyon, Zion, Canyonlands, any of the Southwest's most stunning visual landscapes, hold up a postcard of a desert waterfall, and rasp, "How do I get here?" Rangers smile pityingly and grimace a reply, "Well, it's a twenty-six-mile drive on a washboard, four-wheel-drive road to a ten-mile, overnight hike on an unmarked trail. . . ." As the remaining light drains from the parched visitors' eyes, they glance at their street shoes, then out the window at the sedan, hang their heads and mumble a heavy, "Never mind." It's the same passion: rangers will come back in a body cast to get to these same places. (By the way, never trust a backcountry ranger who isn't beat to shit.)

In the dry sand along the watercourse we find the S-ing print of snake. Between trickling waterways, water striders dimple small pools and cast orbiting shadows on the sandy bottom. We sit for a while in the coolness under pines, and the silver sound of water moving gently over rock, the smell of wet sand—not muddy but fresh and clean—restores us. The water pulls a cool breeze downstream as canyon tree frogs plop into sunlit pools flashing their under-thighs, the bright yellow of tinctured sunflower.

Climbing out of Left Fork and up the long, wide, sand-filled saddle that separates it from Right Fork, we battle prickly scrub oak, heat, and the sun's glare to reach the top, where we see, in all directions, the spectacular result of water running downhill. In this country of open rock and sandy soil, not much holds the place in place. Water falling from the sky finds little purchase and funnels from crack to fracture, rill to canyonette, flowing in sheets and waterfalls downward, ever downward, gaining speed and bulk, until bursting through narrow canyons with the force to move mountains. Geologists use terms such as "instantaneous discharge," where we say flash flood; both are pretty descriptive if you ask me, although saying "I saw an instantaneous discharge yesterday," does sound a tad clinical, or medical, or sexual, I'm not sure which. When applied to canyons, it translates into "Run for your life."

Geologists think canyons deepen during the increased flow of flash floods when water is able to pick up sediment—sand, boulders, rusted cars—

and hurl it downstream, scouring bedrock. Cataclysm, or at least punctuated equilibrium, versus uniformitarianism. (I'm glad for that change; I hated spelling *uniformitarianism* on exams.) One good flood can remove much more sediment than a year's normal flow.

One last blind rappel down a long scrabbly slope, and we're in. The world we came from is beyond reach miles behind and thousands of feet overhead, though we can almost touch both canyon walls with outstretched arms. In the dark coolness of overhung cliffs, there's a delicacy of sound and light and touch. Above, violet-green swallows and black-throated swifts titter on fluttering wings. Our flesh ripples with goose bumps in this remote aloneness where sandstone, the color of skin and as smooth, echoes the quiet resound of water. Our revelry is broken by a shout as one of our party encounters the legendary and much-feared Black Pool.

There's something like this on every good adventure, a renowned, almost mythical obstacle, its notoriety existing, it seems, only to up the ante. On the Colorado River, it's Lava Falls; in Right Fork, it's the Black Pool. In most cases, its reputation exceeds it. We were told the Black Pool would be icy, colder than cold, in Right Fork's sunless depths, a frigid and unavoidable swim at least twenty-five-feet long, around blind, sinuous curves through opaque waters. It was bottomless, they said, and could easily take the unwary backpacked hiker to a cold and silent death.

Well, they're right. We hem and haw. Kick a few stones. Janet, having lugged her inflatable air mattress the entire way and determined to use it, sits, blows it up, plunks her pack aboard, and lunges into the pool, kicking for all she's worth. She's quickly around the first bend and beyond sight, but her ice-blue language reverberating through Zion's inner sanctum assures us she's vibrantly alive. The rest of us discover a route up the left wall and around the pool on a ledge, with only a short rappel into waist-deep water at the end.

Because three of us are inexperienced in rappelling—especially over dry waterfalls where no rock wall lends spin-stopping footholds, supports flailing feet, or eases that dangling-in-the-breeze sensation—the group progresses slowly. We discuss each rappel in agonizing detail, and each time the three finally eschew nerves, grit teeth, and step back over the edge, eyes wide, a dentist-chair grip on the rope. We dangle over broken precipices; spin over resistant, midstream ledges; and slither under and over massive, big-as-a-small-house, canyon-choking boulders. We clamber over broken, wedged ponderosa logs; wade thigh-deep, muck-bottomed puddles; and stumble over the rock-strewn stream course with mud-caked boots; grinning till our faces hurt.

Late in the day, life changes. I go over a twenty-foot pouroff first, unsaddle my pack, and assist from below as the others free rappel, dangling and twisting in their slow descent to the sandy-bottomed wash. While waiting, my eyes course up and over the rock lip, along the fifteen-hundred-foot cliff line past full-size ponderosa pines jutting minisculely from crevices until my gaze stops at the sky overhead, no longer the azure of summer but the depthless black of monsoon. Under overhung canyon walls, all eyes focused on feet and rock, brains performing feasibility studies on a single misstep's possible outcomes, we'd forgotten to look up. Every nerve in my body now jumps, and I yell, "RUN!" just as the first pelting raindrops slap the sand at my feet.

I once read that cockroaches do not need to think about running when someone flicks on the kitchen light. Light sensors on their legs trigger, and their legs run, carrying them mindlessly toward the nearest concealing darkness. In the time it takes to think about running and where, a human can home in for the kill. Talk about your evolutionary adaptation. Something like this kicks in now, and before I can think, I shoulder my pack and run heavily downstream. My mind races, claws at every line on the sheer cliff for purchase, analyses every toehold, calculates every crack for depth above waterline, how many people it can hold, how far up it goes. The rain begins now in earnest, stinging and cold, hitting like something unleashed. My legs keep running, and I with them until something stops me before a shin-high, stream-blocking boulder.

Peering over it, I see an overhung fifteen-foot rappel into a sand-blown hollow. We have to buzz this rappel like Green Berets from a helicopter, but the rope, and my friends, are still tied to the last pouroff. I calculate the bone-breaking probabilities of jumping, and pull back. I look right: as close as a shadow and as unrelenting juts the fifteen-hundred-foot cliff's baby-butt smoothness. I look left: a rockfall blackened with moss hugs the canyon wall like a hundred-foot stairway. My legs run up it, clambering over boulders, slipping on the now-wet stone. I reach the top, my hands muddy and sore, and stand on a life-saving, two-foot ledge crammed against the sandstone cliff and overhung by a foot-wide blind arch—just enough room for six to stand shoulder-to-shoulder. I take my first breath since leaving the last rappel. I do not consider how long we—or, I should say, they—will have to stand here, nor do I consider the terror that is to come. My only concern is getting off the canyon floor.

A hundred feet below me, Marta, the first of the five, skids to a stop and stares wild-eyed over the pouroff. I yell, and she turns, scrambles up the rockfall. One by one the scene replays, until we all stand, soaking in the now-pouring rain, heaving and wide-eyed, backs against the wall. The precipitation turns from a hard rain into a cloudburst and sets overhead with the gray determination of concrete.

We each silently ponder rivulets forming along the arc's lip, shivering as they stream over our shoulders and dribble down our wet T-shirts. I look up and watch the rain coursing down the wall's sandstone sheerness like snowflakes in a speeding car's headlights. It is late afternoon. We are wet. And cold. It is not going to stop raining, and we are not safe.

Jon and I determine to scout ahead for a better place to spend the night; we can't stand here that long. We aren't sure how far the ledge goes, if it stays high or might lead out of the canyon. We head off downstream, jump a dry chute slotted in the canyon wall, and discover within ten feet that the trail heads straight down a brushy slope back to the streambed; it's just a route around the pouroff. We turn back, but the chute is now a waterfall, spitting rock, pine needles, and tree branches. I force a handhold on the other side, but my hand slips on the icy rime forming in the rain-turned-hail and my

Floating rock, Zion Narrows

arm is pushed away by the waterfall's force. I yell for the others, but they can't hear, because at this moment the flood hits. Below, in the streambed, the proverbial fifteen-foot-high wall of water does not bother to fall over the pouroff, but shoots straight out as if shot from a high-pressure hose. It lands thirty feet down canyon and splays against the canyon floor. It has been all of five minutes since I ran screaming from the bottom of the last pouroff. There was no buildup, no warning trickle of ankle-deep water, no freight-train roar. Just a fifteen-foot instantaneous discharge capable of stripping flesh from bone.

Jon and I move back from the waterfall chute and dig our butts into the wooded but meager hillside's soft duff. Jon pulls a nonwaterproof tarp from his pack, and we hunch under its illusory protection. The pouring rain rips boulders loose from the cliff above, and they crash around us with a dull, neck-snapping thud. Thunder smashes into the canyon, and I gain some insight into what a nail must hear when struck. Lightning ricochets off canyon walls. Trees swirl overhead in a blender of motion; branches crack and fall like spears, their broken ends thunk into the soil, sending a shower of leaves and branches against the tarp. That's the backbreaking straw: the terror overtakes me and I jump up and yell over the flood's roar, "We've GOT to get OUT of HERE!" Jon looks at me from beneath the dripping tarp and yells back, "HOW?" I look toward the only exit. Fifty feet downstream the canyon takes an abrupt left turn along a sheer wall where a hanging canyon enters from the right, its lip a hundred feet above the canyon floor. There, in the failing light, I see a cataclysm of water. From where it hits the canyon floor, the flash flood arcs twenty feet into the air. To the right, a waterfall suddenly splurts from the hanging canyon. The two floods collide against the sheer wall, merge and arc fifty feet left, removing, when they collectively hit the canyon floor, 366 truckloads of sediment in five seconds flat. Suppressing every screaming nerve fiber in my being, I bend my body—turgid with adrenaline—bow my head and wordlessly resume my position under the tarp. I am thinking of the headline: "Six Rangers Die as Canyon Widens: Their Mothers Say They Should Have Known Better."

I had long been known, up to this point, to say that I wanted to see a flash flood from a safe place. I can now attest that there is no such thing as seeing a flash flood from a safe place. If you are watching a flash flood, you are in the belly of the beast, part of a digestive process—about to be ejected like so much human waste.

It's now dark. I do not again express my thoughts about our imminent death. I pull my down (read: useless) sleeping bag from my pack, wiggle my legs into it without loosing my "butt-purchase" or dislodging any precious butt-holding soil. One false move and I'm down the slope on a mudslide, a gangly pebble in a debris flow, over a short, straight, handholdless twenty-foot drop into the flood, and whisked away into nothingness.

Remember that joke about the frog in the blender? I'm trying not to. With my heels I dig a footrest and use my head to hold up the soggy but heat-trapping tarp. I fall into a fitful sleep, brimming with crashing trees, falling rock, and howling water. Sometime during the night, the rain ends. I wake to hear the flood rumble unabated in the darkness and wonder when the water will stop, how many days we might be here, and then, how many black pools now lie between us and the last rappel to freedom.

Morning. Light enters the canyon soggily, like a hangover. I am soaked. My sleeping bag is soaked, my pack. Everything I own drips. Wringing out my pack's contents, I discover eggs, potatoes, onions, oil, and miracle of miracles, dry coffee and filters. I wipe off my small backpacker's stove, find a knife. By the time our friends arrive in astonishment (looking, I might add, like a pack of mud wrestlers), Jon and I are eating sizzling eggs and potatoes and drinking hot dark coffee with cream. Why be totally miserable? They look at each other and again at us. Polly says, "We sat awake last night mourning your death! We thought this trail lead right back into the . . . and you're drinking *coffee*!?"

I smile weakly, "Want some?" I proffer the cup.

They stare. Their mouths hang open. "Weren't you worried about *us*?"

To be honest, I hadn't lost much sleep over them. Other things, yes, but them? They, after all, were *rangers*. Jon and I swallow stiffly, mumble something about ranger resourcefulness, and quickly repack—forty pounds heavier for the five gallons of water we carry bound to clothes, packs, sleeping bags.

The flood has stopped. Around the corner we encounter the first lagoon. It's only neck deep where the canyon walls stand four feet apart. We wade it with our packs on—no need to float them on an air mattress now—and use our hands to pull against the undulating canyon walls, the shape of moving water. The cold pool smells slightly of fish, frogs, moss, and dirt, but then so

Slot canyon with flood-wedged log

do we. Flood-rammed logs, as big around as my torso, jam sideways into the canyon twenty feet over our heads.

Less than a half mile from our ringside seats, we enter the Grand Alcove, an immense, echoing amphitheater set into Right Fork's north wall. It's the largest and most beautiful alcove I've ever encountered; people shrink in significance, and we were already feeling pretty small. Massive blocks litter the alcove's sandstone floor, fallen from the ceiling hundreds of feet overhead. Around the back, maidenhair fern and moss spout from alcove seeps, and water darkens the redrock wall. Below, a clear springwater stream cuts its own sinuous mini-narrows: a canyon within a canyon. Slippery redrock cascades tier downstream, and large potholes cup pools. Another time we would sit in its grandeur for hours, but today all we want is out. We zip two rappels fifty feet—no timid climbers today. Within a hundred yards we come to our last major obstacle: Barrier Falls, so named as it creates a seventy-foot barrier to upstream travel.

As we stand at Barrier Falls—with the danger and the Navajo Sandstone narrows at our back, and a flat-floored, half-mile-wide Great West Canyon below—we see, in its openness, not only our original destination for yesterday's camp but also a climber's-eye view of canyon formation. Although narrow canyons are hewn by nature's pressure-washers, how is it that Zion and Great West Canyons are each over a mile wide at their mouths? Beyond a canyon's constricting narrows, even the increased erosive power of Pleistocene runoff or flashing streams no longer reach.

At Barrier Falls we stand precisely at the transition from narrow canyon to wide. In the main canyon, the famous Zion Narrows end abruptly when Zion Canyon flares at the Temple of Sinawava. At that point, one is essentially standing at the same place as at Barrier Falls: at the contact between the Navajo Sandstone above and the Kayenta Formation below. As a river or stream cuts into the homogeneous Navajo Sandstone, it simply makes one big slot, one deep knife-cut. It's not until the river reaches the springline and Kayenta Formation below that the canyon can widen.

Now here's a thing (as they say in Utah)—canyon widening has always been explained like this: The river erodes the softer Kayenta Formation more quickly than the overlying Navajo Sandstone, which leaves the Navajo cliffs unsupported from below. The cliffs then collapse into the canyon, and the river carries away the debris. But you can wander from one end of Zion Canyon to the other and not find any place where the river is undermining the Navajo. The process is correct, the agent only partially: it is water, but it isn't the river; it's the springs.

Zion's springlines have always fascinated me. They occur at approximately the same elevation throughout the canyons, as a line running along the contact between the Navajo and Kayenta. The porous Navajo Sandstone makes a great aquifer. Rain or snow falling on the plateau soaks into the sandstone and percolates down through the cliff, moving between individual sand grains, until it hits a more impermeable layer (called an aquitard or aquiclude); in Zion's case, it's the Kayenta's silty sandstones. When water percolating through the Navajo Sandstone hits the Kayenta Formation, it emerges from the cliff as a seep or spring.

In the main canyon, the well-known Weeping Rock is the best example. Interestingly, water from Weeping Rock has been dated at about twelve hundred years old, and another spring upstream dates at four thousand years. These ages tell us two things: they give some idea of how long it might take water to travel from cliff top to bottom and emerge as a spring, and they explain why these springs don't dry up—because the water that supplies them fell quite some time ago. Hydrologists refer to this water as "fossil water" since it is so old and since, like fossil fuel, it is not easily or quickly replenished.

In one of those beauty-of-nature's-design scenarios, the Navajo's precious desert waters are slowly meted out to obligate spring users such as monkey flower, shooting star, and golden columbine. If the springs dry up, so too the desert's diversity. At Grand Canyon, a study revealed that species concentration at springs is five hundred times greater than in surrounding dry lands, making them not only hot spots of diversity but also the proverbial oasis-in-the-desert for such wide-ranging wildlife as bighorn. Researchers discovered that canyon-bottom springs, vulnerable to repeated scouring (as we witnessed all too closely), support an ephemeral biology, one that re-creates itself after each life-changing flash flood.

Cliff springs, protected from such violence, provide the time and stability needed for new species to evolve, for a biology unique—in the word's true sense—to place, even to a specific spring. For example, the Zion snail (*Physa zionis*) is entirely endemic (native) to two vertical sandstone springs, one in the Zion Narrows and another in the upstream tributary Orderville Canyon.

Spring at Menu Falls

The snail, shell and all, is about this big: ☺. Snails may have been more widespread during the wetter periods after the last glaciation, but as climate warmed and dried, remnant populations held on only at isolated springs. Over time, disparate populations evolved into separate species such as the Kanab ambersnail (*Oxyloma haydeni kanabensis*) found at Grand Canyon's Vaseys Paradise. The issue with such creatures is that one event could wipe out the entire species.

Microscopic snails might not seem very important, but they are an excellent example of a larger problem: most species are becoming snails. As habitats and their connections continue to shrink and disappear, such animals as gray wolves, California condors, native elk, Merriam's turkey, and bighorn are confined to increasingly isolated microhabitats. All these animals once existed at Zion and have been extirpated (made locally extinct). Some have been reintroduced, but we've yet to see whether they will survive long-term or fall prey to the same conditions that initially caused their loss. A recent study revealed that numerous large mammal species continue to disappear from our western national parks, even with protection. Another study disclosed that there is not a reserve on the planet big enough for a new large mammal to evolve. We may find our evolutionary future limited to such microenvironments as petri dishes, the guts of Asian birds, or Zion's remote and protected springs.

I vote for the hallowed sound of water dripping, echoing, pouring from springlines in narrow redrock canyons. But a preserved spring is more than a fenced pool: it takes a park. A single healthy spring is the focal point of immense geological processes, including climate, an extensive regional watershed, and a vast aquifer. Combine these with intact microscopic processes such as biofilms (biofilms? We'll come back to that) and human activities that do no harm, and a spring may retain its natural ecology. But, in actuality, it takes more than a park; it takes a planet.

And, yes, those same springlines influence canyon formation. The Kayenta Formation is indeed softer than the Navajo, though it is eroded not from the river below, but from the springlines above. Springlines at the Navajo's base become zones of weakness where water's incessant drip slowly dissolves the Kayenta's crumbly shales, which then fall away, leaving the upper Navajo cliffs unsupported. The upper cliffs eventually shear along internal vertical fractures and collapse into the canyon. The river or ephemeral stream then works over millennia to carry away the debris. Higher up on canyon walls, rain pries cracks, frost heaves, mudslides ho, gravity pulls, and rocks fall, widening the upper canyon walls even more. Things fall apart.

We rappel Barrier Falls' seventy feet like old pros, amazed that the water pouring over its lip runs clear. It's an easy rappel; the toes of our muddy boots fit nicely into the Kayenta's thin, cascading layers the color of burnt sandstone. The flood has nicely flattened all vegetation three yards back from today's sweetly babbling brook, which makes walking quite pleasant (except for the boot-sucking mud). But it's a long six miles out with water-logged packs and sand-filled shorts. We hardly notice the beauty of Double Falls or the many sparkling pools and waterfalls created by the Kayenta Formation's alternating soft siltstones, mudstones, and resistant sandstones.

Below the Kayenta, Great West Canyon opens out into a flat-footed trudge. No glistening slickrock here, no canyon wren's sweet cascade, no hidden spring's echoing drip. Just sand and sage and the sound of two feet walking. This canyon's flat floor makes it look more like a glacier-carved valley than a stream-carved canyon: U-shaped, not V-shaped. Zion Canyon itself is also U-shaped. I wondered about this for years before consulting Wayne Hamilton, Zion geologist extraordinaire. Wayne reminded me that many of Zion's canyons were once dammed.

A spectacular example lies in Zion Canyon between Canyon Junction and the Court of the Patriarchs. Sometime around eight thousand years ago an immense sandstone fin peeled from the peak known now as "The Sentinel." As it fell two thousand feet into the canyon, the rock pulverized itself and now stands as extremely steep, six-hundred-foot-tall red slopes nowhere near a settled angle of repose. The main canyon road winds its way over a mile through and atop its rubble. This rockfall was so immense, it blocked the canyon completely and dammed the Virgin River. A vast lake pooled upstream from the rockfall, stretching from the Court of the Patriarchs almost to the scenic drive's end, five miles up canyon. The lake existed for some four thousand years and, at its greatest extent, was at least 350 feet deep and left behind sediments 300 feet thick on which the upper canyon road and Zion Lodge now stand. Without this lake and its flat-as-a-lake-bottom deposits, Zion Canyon might be steep walled, rocky, and difficult to access. Great West, too, was dammed near Trail Canyon at least twice, once by lava and later by rockfall.

These lakes fascinate me because we often assume a place has always, at least within a human timescale, looked pretty much as it does now. But eight thousand years ago, when The Sentinel thundered into Zion Canyon, people lived hereabouts. How did this tremendous change affect them? It has certainly affected everyone since. The massive lake probably prevented settlement in Zion Canyon for thousands of years, but after the lake drained, its sediments provided a flat living surface for prehistoric farmers, pioneers, and today's visitors. Geology, for me, can be a pretty inaccessible topic, all those millions of years seemingly infinitely divided into inscrutable time periods such as the Mesozoic, Cretaceous, and Maastrichtian. But give me a good rocks-and-people story, like "Boulder Smashes House" or "Single Rockfall Changes the Known World," and I'm hooked.

Near where the trail leaves Great West, we meet what for us is the ultimate irony: our ranger colleagues coming to search for human remains—ours. They're astonished to see us alive and walking, and we're surprised to see them. The rules of southern Utah and ranger etiquette don't allow for much more than a handshake in these situations. And, although no one will say it, we are grateful—if a tad embarrassed—that our friends have come looking for us. They tell us our flood closed Highway 9, topping the bridge for the first time in living memory. We all marvel at the probabilities of finding that rockfall precisely the instant we needed it; had we been anywhere else in that canyon, our collective and indistinguishable body parts would now be en route to Lake Mead. This death threat may seem overblown, but sixty-seven people have died in Utah flash floods, nine in Zion alone.

We discuss the forecast, checked when we got our permit: clear skies, some chance of clouds; Zion Narrows Danger Level: Moderate. But monsoons in the Southwest do not bother with forecasts. Yesterday a cumulonimbus cloud rose over Zion, sucked moisture from several nearby states and a couple foreign countries, and deposited it in Right Fork of North Creek.

Although we have come to think of monsoons as a time of exceptionally wet weather, in Arabic—that most desert-inspired of languages (from which we also adopted *adobe, coffee,* and my personal favorite, *mocha)*—the word *mausim,* from which *monsoon* is derived, means "season." So technically we have a dry monsoon and a wet monsoon. But in the weather business, monsoon has come to mean a direct wind reversal that changes weather; it was originally applied to Arabian Sea winds that blow for six months from the southwest, drenching southern Asia, and six months from the northwest, toasting the same lands. In the southwestern United States a similar reversal, called the Arizona, Mexican, or Southwest Monsoon, occurs.

During the Southwest dry monsoon, from November to March, cool winds arrive off the Pacific and lose much of their moisture over the Sierra Nevada and mountain ranges of the Basin and Range before arriving in southern Utah, showering Zion with occasional gentle rain. The sky bruises and swells, "occasional gentle rains" can last for weeks, and we desert rats feel like slitting our wrists. But mostly it's dry, brisk, and golden.

During the wet monsoon, July through September, warm, humid air arrives from the Gulfs of California and Mexico and, in the typical pattern, drenches the desert with daily afternoon thunderstorms. Summer arrives regardless of the calendar, when "summer clouds" heave into view one day, littering the sky like wadded tissue. Then, when the real monsoon arrives (using the southern Utah meaning: "thunderstorms"), gigantic anvil-headed clouds, great cliffs of clouds, explode thousands of feet skyward, blacken, send forth lightning, a pestilence of thunder; and sudden rains beat solid rock into submission. Between mausims, Utah's famous cloudless turquoise skies preside over fall and spring. At least, that's how it's supposed to work.

Zion, however, sits precisely at the monsoon's western extent. When that boundary shifts, so too does the weather: some years thunderstorms excavate entire new canyon systems, and other years summer rains never come. Zion's location on the monsoon's edge also means that more of its annual precipitation arrives in winter than summer. Canyonlands and Arches, near Moab, Utah—national parks with elevations and rainfall similar to Zion's—lie within the monsoon boundary and thus receive their annual precipitation about equally distributed between summer and winter. It is a small difference with great effect.

Winter's slow rains tend to soak more deeply into the soil, benefiting deeply rooted plants such as shrubs and trees. Summer rains flash across the soil, aiding shallow-rooted species, forbs, for instance. Thus winter rains create different plant (and thus animal) communities than summer-shifted precipitation. Further, different plant species use water at different times. That way, one species or another will survive no matter when it rains. Ingenious.

But some plants use water *only* during certain seasons; if rains arrive at the wrong time, these plants ignore it. That's one reason environments can differ: the seemingly inconsequential difference of when rain falls.

Now for the kicker: scientists anticipate that global climate change will not only shift (is shifting, has shifted) the monsoon boundary, but also has/is/will affect seasonal precipitation. The U.S. Geological Survey states that a switch to a drier climate, particularly reduced winter rainfall, will reduce groundwater recharge (there go our vibrant springs and rare snails), lessen perennial stream water (bye-bye native fish), increase strong winds and dust storms, weaken biological soil crusts (erosion), reduce plant cover and change species composition, remobilize sand from stable dunes, and increase forest and range fires.

What will this mean for us humans besides having to dust more often? In Zion, reduced winter rainfall will shift vegetation boundaries; different species will invade and replace the Colorado Plateau species we've come to know and love. Economic plants such as ponderosa pine (lumber) will survive only in the smaller acreages available at higher elevations; piñon and juniper might die off or move to higher elevations, leaving lower elevations to heat-adapted species, creosote bush for example. Grasslands will fill not with native grasses, but with such useless invasive exotics as unpalatable cheatgrass (there goes the wildlife neighborhood). The lifestyle and economy we've based on the present regime will change—drastically.

With luck, there will be time for us to change with it—for ranchers to learn new skills, for farmers to switch to crops adapted to hotter, dryer summers. Less water might mean mass human movement away, just as it did for Anasazi and pioneer alike. The species Zion National Park hoped to protect will be gone—moved or dead. It's something managers have never confronted before: their park up and moving away. If we hope to protect a certain species, we may have to set aside lands now where we think that species might end up later. Bizarre to be sure, but also necessary if we hope to plan for the future. This is not idle speculation. Scientists who study butterflies are already predicting that with climate change, the monarch's Mexican refuge will be too cold and wet for the species to survive the winter. Can you imagine a summer without monarchs? I don't want to.

All these dire predictions remind me of pre–Hurricane Katrina warnings of what New Orleans would experience after being hit by a massive hurricane whipped to a frenzy by global warming: broken levees, flooded wards, stranded populations, decimated wetlands. The preceding forecast is the Southwestern version of Hurricane Katrina—a list of things that will change so slowly we won't notice until they hit us unprepared and head-on.

A recent climate study predicts that at our current rate, atmospheric carbon dioxide concentrations will double from preindustrial levels by 2070, triple by 2120, and quadruple by 2160. The study predicts "profound transformations; some potentially beneficial, but many disruptive. Climate zones will shift hundreds of miles north."

It's true that the Zion we see today is just one data point on an evolving continuum. Zion has always changed; that's the one constant. But now, we're the agent and we're moving too fast. At one time a large forest covered Zion and extended to Grand Canyon's lowest level; as ancient climate changed, so too did the forest. The difference was that the transition happened slowly, giving plants and animals time to adapt. But when climate change happens quickly, well, ask the dinosaurs how well that worked for them.

It's easy to feel powerless against such overwhelming forces. But the real take-home message is act now. The longer we wait, the worse the consequences.

And, I wonder, what will we call Zion then? The part that moved away, or the dry canyon walls?

Zion's story

I'm lying back on a fallen sandstone slab, eyes closed, sun on face. The autumn breeze billows around me, and cottonwoods along the Virgin River applaud the day's perfection with a yellow rustle. To my right another slab towers, implanted vertically by its plunge into Zion Canyon, its skin thick with the patina of time, dark moss, yellow lichen.

I hear the clack of rock on rock in the wash below and open an eye to see a young mule deer, her ears and tail flicking gnats, ambling on delicate feet between boulders. Unbound by time, current or ancient, slow or fast, for her

Mouth of Zion Canyon

there is only now. Gnat time. Cooling time. The yellow time of sunflowers and goldenrod. Her dun coat blends the color of grass and stone. I scan the entire bowl of sky to find only a small cluster of clouds like ripples on the river's bottom—otherwise the sky in the south, lazuli; to the north, mountain bluebird. Last time I walked here under a kingfisher sky.

In that dawn, claret cup and cliffs burned in the sun's first unoccluded rays of summer. I hiked to the rock as kingfisher skirted the river's bank, his wings lost in daybreak's blue-gray. Before me, a small crowd gathered to watch the rock mark time.

Just as the sun rimmed the canyon's eastern wall, a shadow exactly the shape, and close to the size, of a howling coyote leapt onto the standing rock. Ears up, front legs stiff, head thrown back, mouth wide, the coyote eats time. The crowd oohed and aahed, then grew silent as the shadow, over the next hour, descended the rock, mouth open, gulping five small petroglyphs: first a figure whose name or story is lost to our knowledge; then a bird's footprint; then a spiral; next the hand-pecked form of a canine; and last another bird print. Only at dawn on this one day, June 21, the summer solstice, does the coyote take shape. And only on this day does redrock reverberate with the clock's sole tick.

This solstice marker, set in motion perhaps a millenium ago by the Virgin Anasazi, is a case of fortuitous geology. Some eons ago, huge rock slabs fell hundreds of feet from the Springdale Member of the Moenave Formation; they landed in a creative jumble that, when the sun rises over its northernmost point on the redrock skyline, casts a shadow from one rock onto

Petroglyph

another which resembles a howling canid. Some few thousand years later, someone noticed the effect, took time to peck symbols into solid stone to mark the spot, and activated a perpetual time machine that will only wind down as time erodes bedrock or planetary orbits change. To what did this soundless alarm, going off, call people?

As the Virgin Anasazi transitioned from hunter-gatherers to semisedentary farmers, a calendar would have placed the people within the year's rotating story. A horizon-based calendar still consulted on the Hopi Reservation in Arizona links sunrise alignments before the solstice with farming chores—field clearing, early planting—indicating when to prepare regardless of weather. Calendars also compute precise dates of important events so proper ceremonies occur at correct times. It is impossible to date exactly when this clock was wound, or to know definitively if those who consulted it were farmers. We can surmise that they were people who inhabited or visited the canyon repeatedly.

It's an easy walk across the canyon and over the river from the stone clock to a treeless knoll where sacred datura bloom, moon white, and fade in the late day. I walk there as clouds gather and light fails. Globemallow, four-o'clock, and Mormon tea brush my legs as I climb the short hill. The view from the top is surprisingly robust: south all the way to Eagle Crags and Smithsonian Butte; up canyon to the Sentinel Slide, and beyond to Lady Mountain; and canyon wall to wall—the Watchman towers overhead; West Temple across the canyon. Near the knoll's north end, in the lee of a large boulder, thin sandstone blocks, set on edge, trace two ancient rooms.

This Virgin Anasazi site—constructed and augmented between AD 700 and 900 and again from AD 1010 to 1300—consists of two storage rooms, three storage cists, and two hearths. This hilltop probably served as flood-safe storage for a stone and adobe dwelling below, closer to the river and now invisible. No foodstuffs remain within the room blocks, so it's not known if these people were farming the Virgin's floodplain, relying on a natural regimen, or creating a mixed economy of agriculture and wild resources.

Most archaeological features in Zion Canyon don't represent long-term living places. This may be a case of unfortunate geology. The forces that contributed to our tumultuous night in Great West Canyon also made and make Zion Canyon a rather unsuitable living place. Zion's archaeological sites are primarily work sites for the seasonally sedentary Anasazi.

Prehistorically, lower Zion Canyon could feasibly support only a small family group, fewer than twenty people. This was a time when natural forage was probably still plentiful and individual families dispersed across the landscape, hunting, gathering seasonal edibles, and gardening small plots. They may have returned to their durable Zion Canyon homestead during specific seasons or multiyear periods; if conditions were especially conducive, they may have spent a lifetime in place.

There is not much we can state definitively anymore. The deeper we study any subject, the more we confront exceptions, nuances, and unexpected new information. Archaeologists now recognize there was no real culture we can name exclusively Anasazi, and they are fine-tuning their language. Even the word Anasazi is out, replaced by the generic term, Ancestral Puebloan.

(I use Virgin Anasazi for readers who wish to learn more about Zion's cultures; looking up "Virgin Ancestral Puebloan" would be fruitless.)

We don't know what the Anasazi called themselves; it's doubtful they had one unifying name for the entire people. They, like us, may have had names for various groups (Rockvilleans, Springdaleans, New Yorkers, and so forth), just as the extant Puebloans do today (Hopi, Zuni, Jemez). Saying Anasazi is like saying American. We can characterize related traits and lifestyles—corn production, pottery, basketry techniques—as Anasazi, but localized technologies were a mix of adaptations dependent on immediate environment and each people's history. We could say that there were myriad ethnicities within an overarching lifeway. Archaeologists have long designated the Anasazi centered on southwestern Utah the Virgin Branch. We should probably address these knoll people as the Zion Canyon Branch of the Virgin Branch of the Anasazi. The "Zionsazi," as endemic as Zion snails, carefully adapted to Zion Canyon's very particular environment.

The knoll people adjusted to Zion by capitalizing on every part of the available environment, then seeking greener pastures, so to speak. I had always assumed that planting and reaping were easier than hunting and gathering, but it turns out I'm wrong. Collecting wild plants was not only easier than tending crops; natural fare also provided more calories. Cattail pollen and roots, pine nuts, bulrush seed, wild rye, acorns, four-wing saltbush, mutton grass (*Poa fendleriana*), sunflower, and Indian rice grass all provide better caloric gain than agricultural crops. Many scientists now reason that people resorted to farming only when native foods were scarce. Thus, finding corn in early archaeological sites may indicate environmental stress—that is, that an area's natural sustenance was impaired by climate change or over-harvest.

During the time the knoll wasn't used, between AD 966 and 1010, conditions in Zion Canyon were unusually parched; some years the Virgin River may have run dry. From AD 1015 to 1100 moisture returned, until the notorious southwest-wide drought sizzled from AD 1125 to 1150. During the first drought, people may have clustered near reliable water and cultivated gardens. As the rains returned, they expanded garden plots to large-scale agriculture, and relied almost totally on the holy trinity of prehistoric agronomy: corn, beans, and squash. The population increased, and when the AD 1125 drought arrived, there were too many people to support with any mix of available economies. As the climate changed, the lifeway so scrupulously tailored to a particular environment no longer worked; and, as many of us have experienced, inventing a new lifeway under stress is difficult, if not impossible.

Thus, by about 1250 the last Anasazi migrated from their former homeland and concentrated along permanent rivers such as New Mexico's Rio Grande. This was the people's standard operating procedure: Times are tough? Leave. But this move catches our eye, so vast and total. The standard explanation: drought. But the people had withstood worse. Researchers now think moisture came, but at the wrong time. Changing climate shifted rain from summer to winter; Anasazi provisions, both natural and agricultural, withered, year after year, until native plants and stored grain were exhausted, and survival lay elsewhere. The future, and the people, relocated where weather dictated. Although we don't understand it yet, this is also our future.

On the hilltop today, coyote scat sits atop a rock, red and seedy, the gut-processed fruit of prickly pear; I think of cactus spines in coyote noses. Exotic, inedible cheatgrass now fills rooms that once stored nutritious rice grass seed. And across the canyon, easily in view, Solstice Rock still beats with annual precision. Each year it marks ceremonies missed, songs unsung. Technology continues without the technologists. To our good fortune, pueblo peoples still sing and dance to the silent chant and rhythm of the seasons, insuring for all the world's people the sun's return to its appointed rounds (thank you). The clock and the carefully ordered rocks on this knoll also serve as placeholder, quietly marking home.

From my knoll-top perch I can't see the slightest indication of the people who followed the Anasazi. For these people, permanent dwellings had little meaning. These were the Southern Paiute, a people who called themselves by many names, each descriptive of a particular group's environment or lifeway. Thus there were, to name a few, the Pagu'its, the fish people, who fished from Panguitch Lake; the Unkaka'niguts, red-cliff-base people, who dwelled near Bryce Canyon; and the Ea'ayekunants, arrow-quiver people, who ranged from the Virgin's headwaters to just below Zion Canyon.

The Numic-speaking Paiute migrated into southern Utah from the Great Basin as early as AD 1000, perhaps overlapping and interacting with our knoll-top Anasazi. The changing climate was pushing the sedentary Anasazi farmers out, and may have impelled the Paiute into southern Utah in search of their own greener pastures. Whenever two cultures overlap, especially during hard times, resource competition ensues. Recent theory suggests that southern Utah's Anasazi may have left as the Paiute increased, or that the two groups melded, each learning important survival techniques from the other.

In and around Zion, Paiute groups integrated into distinct regions centered on a river or spring. For the Ea'ayekunants, it was the Virgin River; for the Unkaka'niguts, it was the Sevier. The Pagu'its relied on Panguitch Lake. These territories, which modern anthropologists call *cultural ecoscapes,* contained what was necessary for each band's self-sufficiency: dependable water for irrigated gardens of maize, squash, and beans (they may have learned farming from the Anasazi); upland forests for elderberry, chokecherry, and mule deer; midland elevations for piñon nuts, sego bulbs, serviceberries, and pronghorn; and lowland deserts for sunflower, grass seed, agave, and rabbit. Brush-shelter villages developed near central water sources, but the Paiute moved throughout their ecoscape seasonally, camping near outlying springs and harvesting wild plants and animals. This may sound similar to early Anasazi technology, and so it may have been. But the Anasazi evolved into homebodies, staying in place, becoming skilled agriculturists; and, as they consolidated into larger and larger stone-built towns, eventually overwhelming local environments and relocating. Anasazi town life, coupled with the intensive land use needed to support it, was ultimately unsustainable.

Both the Virgin Anasazi and the Southern Paiute centered their homelands on one of the Zions. The Anasazi stayed primarily on the lower reaches of the Virgin River's North and East Forks (Zion Canyon), while the Paiute focused on a larger Zion—the biotic Zion—in a sense, participating as members of the ecoscape. They ranged through its elevational gradients and resources in extended families capable of easy seasonal movement, quickly constructing brush shelters. The Paiute lifeway speaks to scale: few possessions, no wealth accumulation, small bands roving the land. I often wonder if this lifeway is a possible future we all share. If so, it might be wise to listen to the Paiute closely.

Just as the extant Puebloans hold rain and what we modern folk call "nature" sacred, so the Paiute hold in reverence their ancestral waters and traditional ecoscapes. They view the land in a way most people do not, believing that everything is alive—air, springs, plants, mountains, minerals, rivers, animals, rocks—and that each must be treated with respect. The Paiute believe their people were put in place, this place, to care not only for nature but also for the spirituality dwelling in the land. The Paiute term for homeland, Puaxante Tevip, translates as "Sacred Land." One way Puaxante Tevip is honored is by speaking directly to the land and its other-than-human inhabitants. Another is the passing on of story and song.

The Paiute lifeway may have continued into the deep future as it had in humanity's deep past, if not for the arrival of another wave of immigrants. The traditional Paiute economy was eventually overwhelmed. Puaxante Tevip was invaded by foreigners, and Paiute waters usurped. Incursion brought starvation, bloodshed, and devastating epidemics from European diseases. Alien creatures—cattle, horses, goats—were unleashed on Puaxante Tevip, decimating Paiute sustenance. Up to 90 percent of Paiutes died after contact.

The Paiutes say they were forced from this land when pioneers settled the only places water made habitable. Even though cut off from their cultural ecoscape, and depleted by disease and hunger, the Paiute survive today as the Paiute Tribes of Utah, Arizona, Nevada, and California. They remain a people deeply connected to Puaxante Tevip. The Southern Paiute still talk to the land. And the land still listens.

It is November, and dusk gathers early. Down canyon, clouds strengthen and what warmth the day held flees. From my knoll top, I can discern, even in the late light, where cottonwood track the river's path and wind green and gold along historic ditches. Just beyond the park boundary, in Springdale, irrigated fields still flush green. Below, campground roads meander through a few remaining pecan and cherry trees seeded by pioneers; old stone walls, two feet high, run back canyons unplanted for generations. Here Zion Canyon is at least a half-mile wide, and accommodatingly flat floored.

From this knoll I can see where my friend J. L. Crawford lived as a child, born in what is now the park in 1914, the spot near park headquarters now subsumed by a campground. It's easy standing here to imagine it; to hear children laughing, to see them running, climbing trees, splashing in the river and watching sticks whirl away on the current. It doesn't matter whose children they are: Anasazi, Paiute, pioneer, kids I know from down the street. People have long lived in Zion Canyon's redrock embrace.

J. L. Crawford is to me a piñon pine, a Utah juniper, as integral a part of the landscape as a cliffrose on a warm spring day. His words are solid as rock. I can imagine him there, a tanned, towheaded youngster, smiling as he does still. I'm willing to bet he told stories even then. J. L. worked for years

J. L. Crawford and Elva Twitchell

as a naturalist and interpreter in Zion National Park, retiring just as I arrived in the early 1980s. There are times I feel my twenty-five years here qualify me as an old-timer, but then I talk to J. L. and realize what a babe-in-the-canyon I am. J. L.'s wonderful wife, Fern, was once so kind as to brand me a "middle-timer," a joke I cherish. J. L.'s stories brim with details almost a hundred years lost to our experience, but still within the mind of a living man.

"I was born in Zion Canyon," J. L. says, "in the little community called Oak Creek, two miles from Springdale in the mouth of Zion Canyon. I lived there until I was seventeen years old. I was born right across from [what's now] the Administration Building, and I had the Temples and Towers of the Virgin to look at. I've heard a lot of people say it's the most outstanding skyline in all the world. Pretty good place to live and be a kid."

He talks about how when he was a young boy, there was no road to Zion from Virgin. We were so isolated," J. L. says. "We couldn't buy things out of a store; we grew everything we ate. In April we'd be out there planting all kinds of vegetables; we had fields of corn, sorghum cane. Course everone had alfalfa fields, and there'd be some wheat planted. My brother had his cow to milk and I had a cow to milk, morning and night. And you know how weeds grow, especially when you irrigate, so we had to hoe, hoe, hoe. Weeding was a lot of work, but you had to do it if you were going to eat." We might call these settlers the Zion Canyon Branch of the Southern Utah Branch of the Pioneers, so specialized to this isolated place they became.

From 1879 to 1933 when the park bought them out, J. L.'s family farmed from what is now the park's Human History Museum to the Springdale

Town Hall. Although they could grow just about anything, except, they tell me, potatoes, the land could only support a few families. "The reason my grandfather went up that canyon to farm? One word explains it . . . water. Without water you don't grow crops and without crops you don't eat. That river was our lifeblood." I imagine J. L. and an Anasazi fellow would have much to talk about.

Elva Twitchell, J. L. Crawford's older sister, and ninety-two when I last talked with her, has a memory sharp as a cliff edge. She says,

> I remember once we went up to the narrows there at the Temple of Sinawava. My folks they all cooked up a big lunch and us kids had a ball playing in the river and running up and down. We had the canyon all to ourselves, just us two families. We never dreamed it'd ever get a highway up in there. Cause that [The Temple of Sinawava] was something we hadn't seen before and I didn't again until they got a road up there. It would take all day to go up [in a buckboard wagon], have our lunch, play around awhile, and come back in time to do the chores and milk the cows.

Other old-timers told me stories of hard times, of two little girls killed when a swing broke, of a toddler drowned in an irrigation ditch, of a young man killed when the rock he shaded beneath rolled. Those stories, for some reason, stay with me. The old pain still fresh on old faces. Their stories make me think of things my hillside's empty room blocks don't tell; of individual Anasazi and Paiute lives; of long-lost stories; the joys and triumphs, the pain and sadness of living in this sacred land.

Both J. L. and Elva well remember the Virgin's rampages.

"Oh, yes," Elva says, "I remember the floods. If it got stormy, cloudy even, up canyon, we stayed away from the river." I wince a bit, and nod. But it wasn't just that. "Those floods could have quite an effect on our crops," Elva says, "because it washed the dams out, then our ditches would be dry. We couldn't water the crops until they put in a new dam."

This is a fact of life in Zion, and in all southwestern canyons. River channels alternately agrade (fill) and erode, providing farmland, then liquidating it. Throughout prehistory, geology aided and plagued Zion's inhabitants. Recent studies show that low streamflows deposit alluvium in canyon bottoms, while increased streamflows following drought carve deep arroyos. This erosion leaves farm fields stranded above the river's irrigating reach. Heavy rain carved arroyos in Zion Canyon twice in the recent past, once between AD 1200 and 1400 and then again from 1883 to 1940. Arroyo cutting coincided with both Anasazi abandonment and the pioneer problems Elva remembers. It may have been the last straw for the few Anasazi still hanging on. But by 1940, pioneers could go to the store.

During the 1700s and 1800s, the Virgin River flowed in fairly well-defined channels overhung by native grasses and riparian vegetation. But in the late 1800s Zion-area streams underwent a catastrophic change. Arroyos sliced through streambeds, in some places up to eighty-feet deep. Then the same channels widened extensively. J. L. and Elva both recall the broad, flat, treeless Virgin where wagons could cross without trouble. But the arroyo-cutting days of their grandparents caused abandonment of early settlements and roads, and destruction of farmlands, dams, reservoirs, and irrigation ditches. Floods and the resulting stream-channel changes undermined the agricultural history of the Zion region. Geology paved the way for farmers ancient and modern. And then geology withdrew consent. Amazing what a little climate change can do.

The Crawford farm lies just below my knoll, the same place the Anasazi farmed eight hundred years ago. Farther up canyon, walls narrow. Tall box elder trees snooze in the fall's cool somnolent evenings while the river, ever restless, swings her hips wide in her bed, first nudging one canyon wall, then the other. It appears that not many folks inhabited Zion Canyon much beyond the Crawford Farm.

If people lived up Zion Canyon before eight thousand years ago, the Sentinel Slide and lake covered any evidence. Between four thousand and eight thousand years ago, upper Zion Canyon's floor would have been three hundred feet under the lake, not an easy place to live, although one National Park Service archaeologist jokes that the Paleo-Indians would have been happy there, sitting on a ledge with their feet up, fishing poles propped, drowning worms in Lake Zion. And it may be that the Anasazi later lived in upper Zion Canyon on prehistoric earthen terraces now eroded by flood-waters, their hoes and stone ax blades now on course to the Pacific. Historic use and flooding may have altered the archaeological record, so that today we find only traces of their presence beyond my knoll.

In the 1860s, three farmers did brave Zion's upper reaches where the only land suitable for agriculture existed upstream from the Court of the Patriarchs: the lake bottom created by the Sentinel Slide.

Isaac Behunin moved to Springdale in January 1862 and built a cabin

Heaps Canyon, winter

near what is now Zion Lodge. William Heaps moved in just across the river north of the Emerald Pools outlet stream, and the polygamist John Rolf moved one wife in just upstream from Heaps, another in what is now the Grotto Picnic Area. Behunin, persecuted with the Mormons as they moved across the country, felt safe in the hard-to-reach, roadless upper canyon, and named it Zion, his haven. He felt that if the Mormons were again harassed, this spectacular and inaccessible canyon could become their place of refuge. (I'm not sure how he thought they would all fit.)

Behunin chose this particular name because the Mormon Church's founder, Joseph Smith, used it in his Doctrine and Covenants, saying that a new group of the Lord's saints would again stand "upon Mount Zion, which shall be the city of New Jerusalem." The "finger of the Lord" pointed Smith to Independence, Missouri, as the New Zion. But unhappy townsfolk chased the Saints from Nauvoo, Illinois, to Independence, Missouri, to the Utah Territory. Many would say the Saints found their Zion in the city they founded, Salt Lake. The word Zion comes from the Bible, the name of one of the hills on which Jerusalem was built. Over the years, the word came not only to denote a place but also to connote an ideal, a promised land.

In 1870, when Mormon president Brigham Young visited southern Utah and Zion, he had a different idea. After a particularly hard journey into the canyon, he supposedly said, "This is *not* Zion." Many of his followers thereafter dutifully called the place Not Zion.

Behunin's Zion only served him a short decade before he moved to Mt. Carmel, Utah, in 1872. Zion's other up-canyon residents, Heap and the

Rolfs, moved to Rockville in 1874. They probably moved on because they were dealing with many of the same issues that had kept the Anasazi out of Zion Canyon a thousand years before: floods, rockfalls, and the short growing season beneath those narrow canyon walls. This was certainly true of the upper Canyon's last resident, Oliver D. Gifford. Gifford farmed in what is now the Grotto Picnic Area. In 1880, he returned from a trip to Springdale to find his spring, field, and a stand of tall pines buried under tons of rock. Above, on the cliff, the freshly broken rock bright, soared a new arch now called the Arch on Red Arch Mountain; they didn't even name it after him.

The history of people in the canyon reveals much about Zion's geology. Just ask Jack Burns. Burns, a resident of Rockville, awoke at 5:35 a.m. on October 11, 2001, to find a boulder the size of two Winnebagos in his bathroom. The impact leveled half his house and sent fractures worthy of the San Andreas through the rest. The collapsing roof stopped a foot above his bed.

In the dark, Burns managed to crawl from bed, pick up the phone (which was dead), and try the door (which was jammed). "I had no idea what happened," he says. "I heard a loud thud. And then—and this all happened in seconds—I heard windows crashing, water running, smoke alarms going off, and felt debris burying me."

Burns shimmied through the (amazingly) intact bedroom window. A neighbor later found him crouched and in shock in the dubious shelter of the home's still-standing back wall. The air outside was filled with thick dust. "That's a smell I'll never forget," he says. "Fresh earth, extremely strong."

The rock, sixteen feet tall by fourteen feet wide and weighing 250 tons, simply peeled off the cliff five hundred feet above, bounced once, and landed on the house. A second 500-ton boulder landed in the front yard. There had been no recent earthquake to rattle loose suspect rocks, no heavy rain to undermine them. It was just another beautiful day in Paradise. It took dynamite to blow Jack's rock out of the house. Although the house was rebuilt, Jack doesn't live there anymore.

Speaking of the San Andreas, two rumpled houses perched on a mesa near Zion's South Entrance attest to the nearness of the Hurricane Fault. An earthquake, registering 5.9 on the Richter Scale, hit at 4:26 a.m. on September 2, 1992. According to the U.S. Geological Survey, it caused one of the largest landslides in the world resulting from a 5.9 quake. The slide closed Highway 9 in Springdale, ruptured power and water lines, and generally surprised the heck out of everybody. It's easy to forget, in this gentle sedimentary landscape, that geology is an active verb.

Everywhere the earth slides away, piles up somewhere else, hardens, then erodes again. Earth's continents, viewed from outer space in quick time would look like one oozing, sloppy mess, continually sliding around the globe, forming and reforming, rather like a giant mud pie slathered by an invisible hand. It's a mess, really, when you think about it. The land refuses to hold still. Geology is an ongoing conversation humans have with a landscape.

My neighbor spent the better part of four years sculpting a garden worthy of *Sunset Magazine,* only to have it completely rearranged one morning by the rampaging Virgin River. We move earth and the earth responds, supporting our actions or denying them. This conversation is no different, though probably less crucial, than the discussion Anasazi and pioneers had with the land. When I began this book Zion was in the midst of a drought, and as I finish, the canyon is lousy with wildflowers and ruined xeriscaped gardens from the wettest year ever recorded. It seems the jet stream or the monsoon boundary has slipped a bit, bringing hefty winter rains. During the 2005 water-year, Zion received over thirty inches of precipitation; an average year sees fourteen. At least the rains will recharge the aquifer and keep canyon springs flowing, replenishing Zion.

The beginning of the cycle is also the end. But that doesn't mean we understand everything that is Zion. Even something as obvious and plain as rock still holds secrets. Harry Kurtz Jr. of Clemson University is only just scratching the surface, or not as the case may be, of the Navajo Sandstone. He studies hidden ecosystems that not only seem to hold the Navajo together, but may also have great effect on aquifers. Say this ten times fast: cryptoendolithic microbial biofilms. Ooh! I just love those big words! (*crypto* = "hidden"; *endo* = "inside"; *lithic* = "rock") These are microbes—Kurtz has identified eight hundred organisms so far—that live in pores between sandstone's individual grains. The microbes create communities by extruding an "extracellular polymeric substance," otherwise known as slime. (I love biospeak.) Many researchers believe that the new science of biofilms will change the way we understand medicine, industry, ecology, and agriculture.

These slimy filaments stick not only to each other, but also to sandstone and to anything useful that floats by in the atmosphere, including nutrients, airborne clay, and pollen. The microbes munch on these organic compounds, and they may also get water from *inside* the rock. Dr. Kurtz hypothesizes that the microbes do this by creating, through their pore-blocking filaments, a biofilm on and just under the sandstone surface that slows water evaporation from the aquifer. The humidity inside the Navajo is as high as 60 to 80 percent; thus, the microbes collect water by precipitating it from the aquifer on the inside of the cliff face! Wow.

Look at a 2,000-foot-tall cliff of Navajo Sandstone. What you don't see are the billions, and billions, and billions, and billions of microorganisms that populate its inner space. These biofilms also strengthen sandstone, hardening it to wind and water erosion. Many of the Southwest's odd formations, usually attributed to rock's differential erosion, in fact may be created by the presence or absence of endolithic biofilms. Kurtz draws two fascinating conclusions from this idea. First, conventional thought has always portrayed microbes as agents of destruction, turning solid rock to soil. But Kurtz thinks that microbes actually slow erosion. Second, the unique landforms created by this biological glue might enhance our ability to detect signs of extant or extinct microbial life on other planets. Amazing.

Speaking of other planets, the Navajo Sandstone recently came in handy in interpreting a Mars mystery. Marjorie Chan of the University of Utah may have solved the problem of blueberries on Mars. Blueberries? In 2004 NASA's Opportunity Rover scooting around the Meridiani Planum of Mars detected gray pebbles loaded with hematite, or iron, dotting the landing site and embedded in nearby rock. Chan had predicted they'd be there: Moqui marbles, iron concretions, just like those that roll over slickrock and pool in depressions in Zion's Navajo Sandstone. Chan thinks Zion's concretions formed twenty-five million years ago, when minerals precipitated from groundwater flowing through the Navajo Sandstone, and that the blueberries of Mars may have formed in a similar manner. Bacteria, it turns out, help concretions form more quickly, and Chan hopes to study Zion's marbles for past microbial activity, which, like Kurtz's microbe-influenced landforms, may help determine if life existed on Mars.

It's dark now. An almost-full moon rises bright and immense over the canyon rim. I have moonbeams aplenty to guide my trek down the knoll. Overhead stars burst from blackness, their camouflaging cloak of daylight gone. I am thinking of the stories of Zion and how they evolve, change, and grow. New languages spring into being, new words, thoughts, ideas, life. Even the oldest stories continue through new tellers. Zion still tells its own stories, and the land, as Clifford Jake would say, is still waiting for our answer.

Now, to the moon's lower left, a fiery bright orb rises, Mars, the red planet—red as a Moqui marble—and rolls around the sky, basking in moonlight as do I. The stories change as do the tellers, but the meaning has always remained the same: *Puaxante Tevip. Zion. Sacred.* I wish I may, I wish I might, have the wish I wish tonight: that Zion will always be that way.

bibliography

Bala, G., K. Caldeira, A. Mirin, M. Wickett, and C. Delire. "Multicentury changes to
the global climate and carbon cycle: Results from a coupled climate and carbon cycle
model." *Journal of Climate* 18, no. 21 (2005): 4531–44.

Chronic, Halka. *Pages of Stone: Geology of Western National Parks and Monuments, Grand
Canyon and the Plateau Country.* Seattle: Mountaineers, 1988.

———. *Roadside Geology of Utah.* Missoula, Mont.: Mountain Press Publishing Company,
1990.

Eves, Robert L. *Water, Rock, and Time: The Geologic Story of Zion National Park.* Springdale,
Utah: Zion Natural History Association, 2005.

Hamilton, Wayne. *The Sculpturing of Zion*. Springdale, Utah: Zion Natural History Association, 1984.

Harrison, Joe J., Raymond J. Turner, Lyrium L. R. Marques, and Howard Ceri. "Biofilms: A new understanding of these microbial communities is driving a revolution that may transform the science of microbiology." *American Scientist* 93, no. 6 (November–December 2005): 508. Also available at www.americanscientist.org.

Hatfield, Sharon, and David Hatfield. *Sacrifice Rock Solar Solstice Marker Project*. Zion National Park Project Report. On file, Zion National Park, Utah, August 23, 1994.

Hereford, Richard, Gordon C. Jacoby, and V. A. S. McCord. *Geomorphic History of the Virgin River in the Zion National Park Area, Southwest Utah*. U.S. Geological Survey Open-File Report 95–515, undated.

Kurtz, Jr., Harry D., R. Cox, and C. Reisch. "A microcosm system for the study of cryptoendolithic microbial biofilms from desert ecosystems." *Biofilms*, 2 (2005): 1–8.

Kurtz, Jr., Harry D., and Dennis I. Netoff. "Stabilization of friable sandstone surfaces in a desiccating, wind-abraded environment of south-central Utah by rock surface microorganisms." *Journal of Arid Environments* 48 (2001): 89–100.

Oral Histories from *Pioneer Voices of Zion Canyon*. Interviews sponsored by the Zion Natural History Association and Zion Canyon Field Institute. Conducted by Greer Chesher, et al. Springdale, Utah: Zion National Park, 2004.

Perkins, S. "Long ride west: Many western sediments came from Appalachians." *Science News* 164 (August 30, 2003): 131–32.

Schroeder, Albert H. *Archeology of Zion Park*. No. 22. Salt Lake City: University of Utah, Department of Anthropology, June 1955.

Siegel, Lee. "Earth has 'blueberries' like Mars." University of Utah News Release, Salt Lake City, June 16, 2004. Available at www.utah.edu/unews/releases/04/jun/marsmarbles.html.

Smith-Cavros, Eileen M. *Pioneer Voices of Zion Canyon*. Photographs by Michael Plyler. Springdale, Utah: Zion Natural History Association, 2006.

Sprinkel, Douglas A., Thomas C. Chidsey, Jr., and Paul B. Anderson, eds. *Geology of Utah's*

Parks and Monuments. Publication 28. Salt Lake City: Utah Geological Association, 2000.

Stoffle, Richard W., Diane E. Austin, David B. Halmo, and Arthur M. Phillips III. *Ethnographic Overview and Assessment: Zion National Park, Utah and Pipe Spring National Monument, Arizona*. Tucson: Bureau of Applied Research in Anthropology, University of Arizona, and Denver: Southern Paiute Consortium, Pipe Spring, Ariz., for Rocky Mountain Regional Office, National Park Service, July 1995.

Varley, Kerry, and Susanne Eskenazi. *The Watchman Site (42WS126) Zion National Park, Utah*. National Park Service and Desert Research Institute Cooperative Agreement Number: CA-1590-9-0001. Las Vegas: Desert Research Institute, December 2002.

Woodbury, Angus M. *A History of Southern Utah and Its National Parks*. Salt Lake City: Utah State Historical Society, 1944. Reprinted 1950.

about the author

Greer Chesher's book *Heart of the Desert Wild: Grand Staircase–Escalante National Monument* won the Utah Book Award for nonfiction. Chesher's other books include *The Desert's Hoodoo Heart: Bryce Canyon National Park; Dinosaur! The Dinosaur National Park Quarry; Bryce Canyon Impressions; National Park Rangers! An Activity and Sticker Book* for kids; and *Moviemaking: Films Made on the Colorado Plateau.* Her naturalist essays have appeared in *Northern Lights, Petroglyph, Canyon Journal,* and *Black Ridge Review,* and in the book *Comeback Wolves: Western Writers Welcome the Wolf Home.* Chesher is half of that daring duo, the Adventure Dogs. With her faithful companion Bo, the border collie, Greer travels the Southwest in search of truth, vision, and a good cup of coffee. She rangered for the National Park Service for twenty years at such places as Zion and Grand Canyon National Parks. She lives in Rockville, Utah, and follows where curiosity leads, writing all the way.

about the photographer

Michael Plyler has been photographing the desert Southwest for nearly thirty years and loving it for even longer. He is the director of the Zion Canyon Field Institute under the auspices of the Zion Natural History Association. Mr. Plyler was awarded one of two prestigious Visual Artist Fellowships from the Utah Arts Council in 1993–94. He has also been photographing Guatemala and the Mayan people there for twenty-five years.

His work has appeared in numerous publications, most recently the new Zion geology book: *Water, Rock, and Time*. His work is held in a variety of public and private collections and has been exhibited widely in this country and abroad. He has received many commissions as well.

Michael's personal work is rendered solely in black and white and he uses large-format cameras and the Ansel Adams zone system to translate his vision. He lives in Springdale, Utah, in Zion Canyon with his wife, Sandy; their dog, Sadie; and Annabel the cat.

Library of Congress Cataloging-in-Publication Data
Chesher, Greer K.
    Zion Canyon : a storied land / text by Greer K. Chesher ;
photographs by Michael Plyler.
        p. cm. – (Desert places)
    Includes bibliographical references.
    ISBN-13: 978-0-8165-2487-7 (pbk. : alk. paper)
    ISBN-10: 0-8165-2487-4 (pbk. : alk. paper)
    1. Zion National Park (Utah)–Description and travel. 2. Zion
National Park (Utah)–Pictorial works. 3. Zion National Park
(Utah)–History. 4. Natural history–Utah–Zion National Park.
5. Desert ecology–Utah–Zion National Park. 6. Natural history–
Utah–Zion National Park–Pictorial works. 7. Desert ecology–
Utah–Zion National Park–Pictorial works. I. Plyler, Michael, 1955–
II. Title.
F832.Z8C48 2007
917.92´480434–dc22   2006030912